HAL•LEONARD
MANDOLIN
PLAY-ALONG

AUDIO
ACCESS
INCLUDED

VOL. 12

T0085477

PLAYBACK+
Speed • Pitch • Balance • Loop

To access audio visit:
www.halleonard.com/mylibrary

Enter Code
5308-7378-2624-3467

Ben Wayson: Mandolin
Bruce King: Mandolin on "Blue Grass Breakdown"
Mark Hembree: Bass, Paul Kienitz: Fiddle, Jon Peik: Banjo & Guitar
Chris Kringel/Kyle White: Sound Engineer

Cover photo by Thomas S. England/The LIFE Images Collection/Getty Images

ISBN 978-1-4950-6591-0

For all works contained herein:
Unauthorized copying, arranging, adapting, recording, Internet posting, public performance,
or other distribution of the music in this publication is an infringement of copyright.
Infringers are liable under the law.

Visit Hal Leonard Online at
www.halleonard.com

Contact us:
Hal Leonard
7777 West Bluemound Road
Milwaukee, WI 53213
Email: info@halleonard.com

In Europe, contact:
Hal Leonard Europe Limited
42 Wigmore Street
Marylebone, London, W1U 2RN
Email: info@halleonardeurope.com

In Australia, contact:
Hal Leonard Australia Pty. Ltd.
4 Lentara Court
Cheltenham, Victoria, 3192 Australia
Email: info@halleonard.com.au

INTRODUCTION

Greetings, mandolin pickers!

Whether you're new to mandolin and feel ready to tackle the music of the Father of Bluegrass, or have been playing for years and want to expand your repertoire and practice soloing with the help of some quality backing tracks, this book/audio set is for you.

Included here are eight choice picks of Bill Monroe's most famous compositions that every bluegrass mandolinist should know, written in standard notation and tab, and recorded by a top-notch band for you to play along with. From the blazing, hillbilly romp of "Blue Grass Breakdown" to the beautiful, pensive piece "My Last Days on Earth," this collection captures the essence of Bill Monroe's unmistakable style.

Bluegrass has forever been an aural tradition, with musicians learning or teaching songs by ear without the aid of notes written down. While learning strictly by ear is a great way to develop solid musicianship for the long run, having notes and tab to read can speed up the learning process greatly! Don't worry, though, you don't have to know how to read music to use this book. Check out the notation legend on page 48 for guidance on reading tablature (tab)—an easy-to-decipher numeric system—and listen to the demo tracks to hear how Monroe's parts are played, note-for-note.

Bluegrass also has a tradition of improvisation where players are free to embellish melodies and develop their own ways of playing in the moment. Most musicians never play a song the same way twice, and Bill Monroe was no exception. Throughout his various studio and live recordings of these tunes, Monroe altered the melodies, phrasing, and mandolin breaks of his songs at will, with the fluidity of a master. In that spirit, we did not try to exactly replicate any of his specific recordings for this play-along, instead allowing the band to get a great feel for you to jam with.

Enjoy!

Big Mon

Words and Music by Bill Monroe

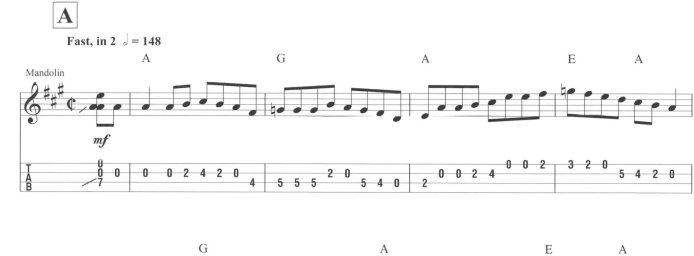

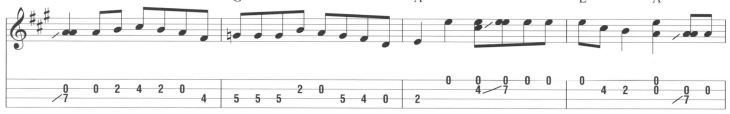

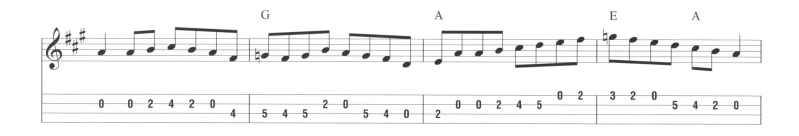

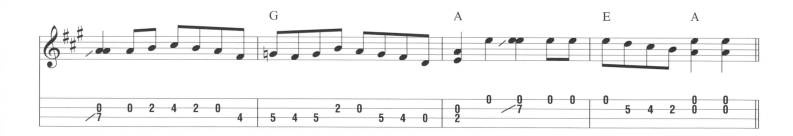

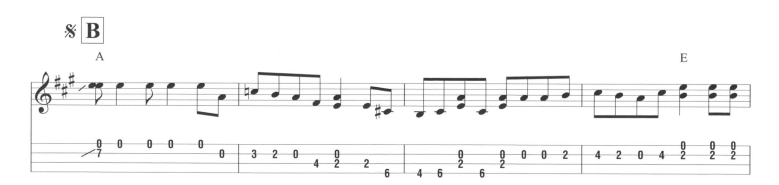

© 1965 (Renewed) UNICHAPPELL MUSIC, INC.
All Rights Reserved   Used by Permission

To Coda ⊕

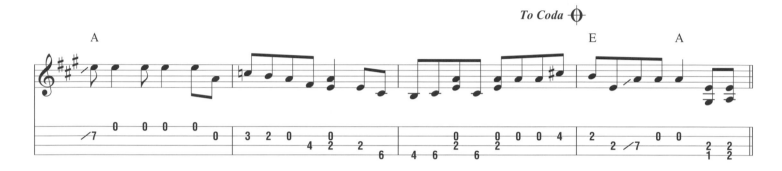

C

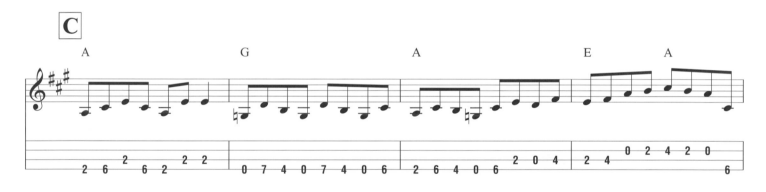

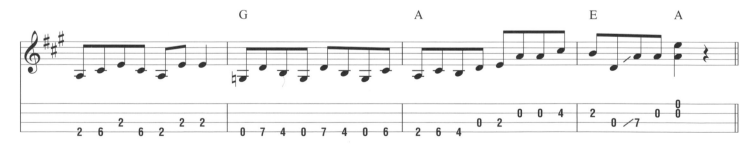

D Banjo

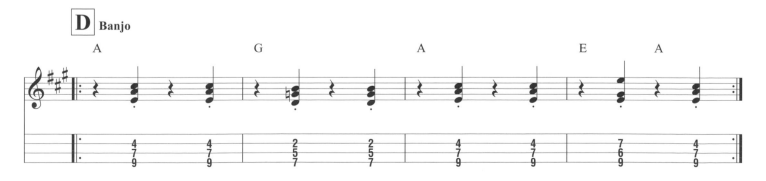

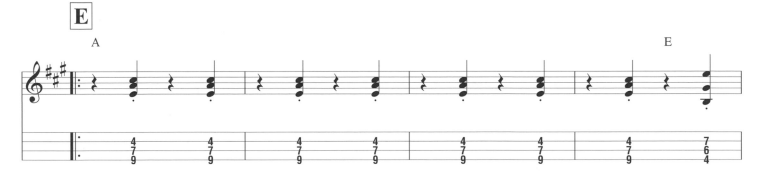

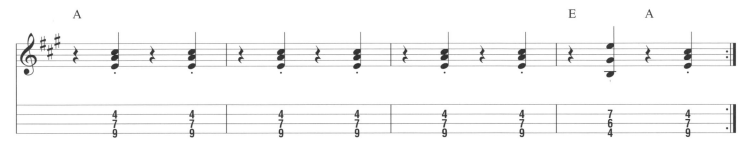

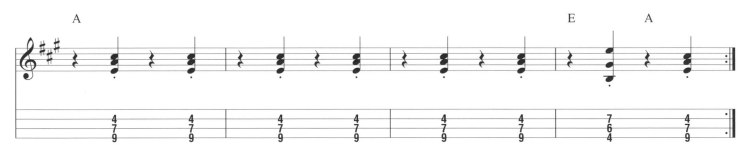

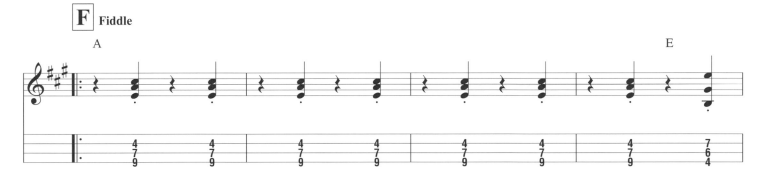

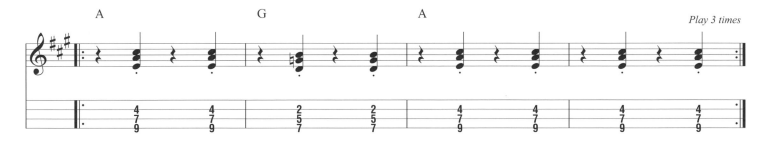

Coda

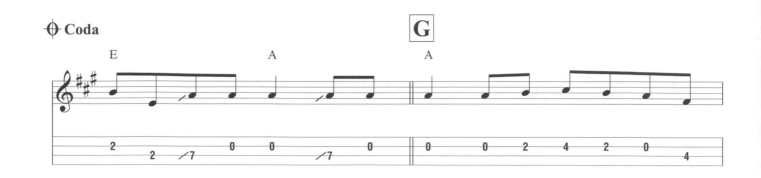

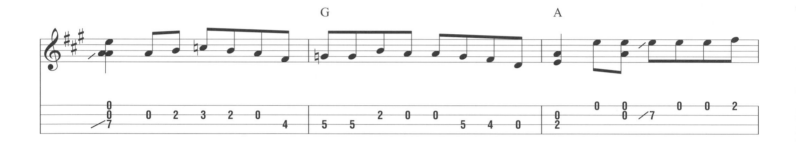

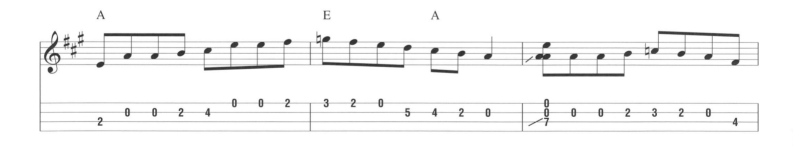

Blue Grass Breakdown

Words and Music by Bill Monroe

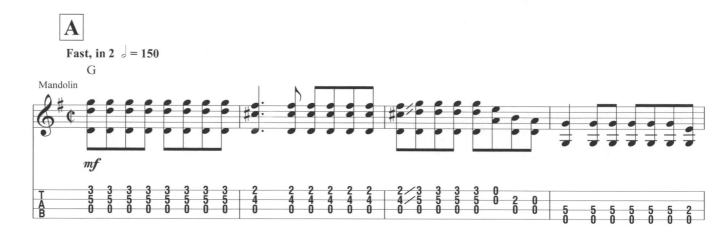

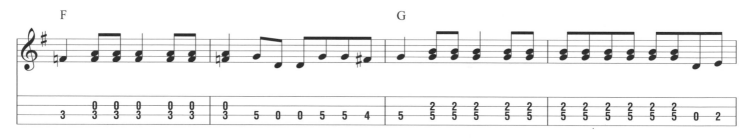

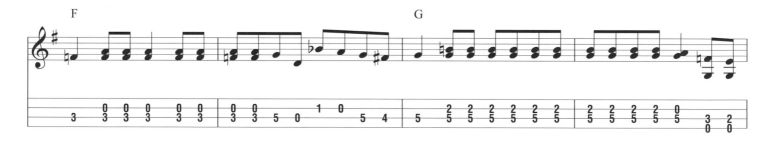

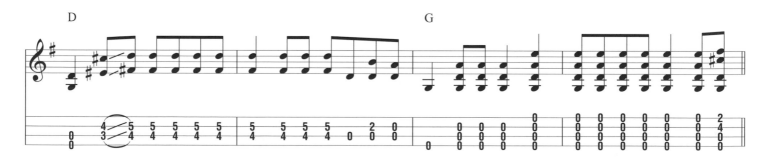

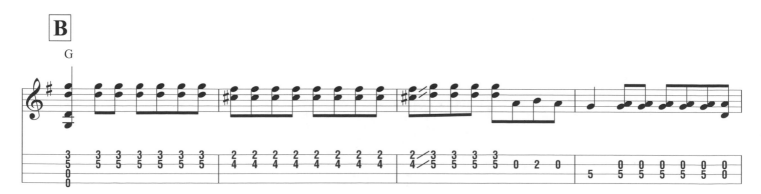

Copyright © 1948 Bill Monroe Music, Inc.
Copyright Renewed
All Rights Administered by BMG Rights Management (US) LLC
All Rights Reserved   Used by Permission

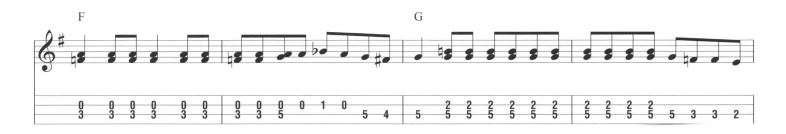

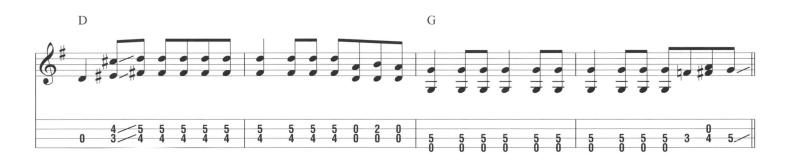

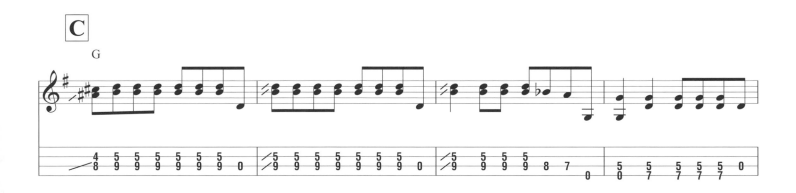

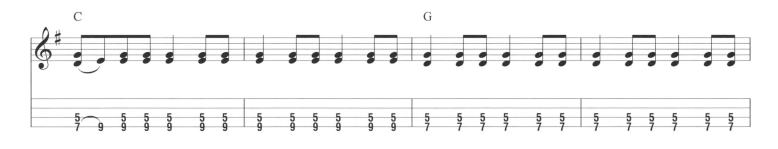

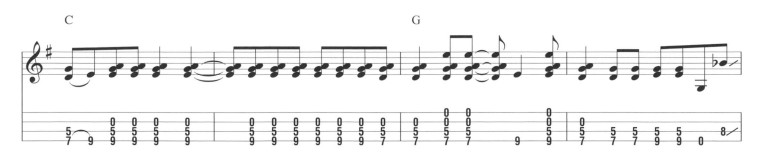

D Banjo

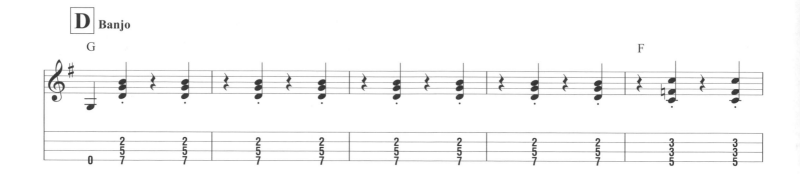

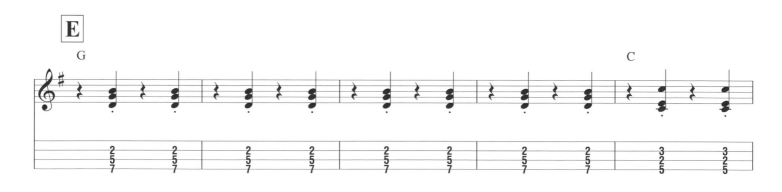

E

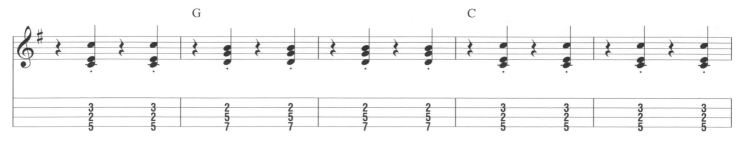

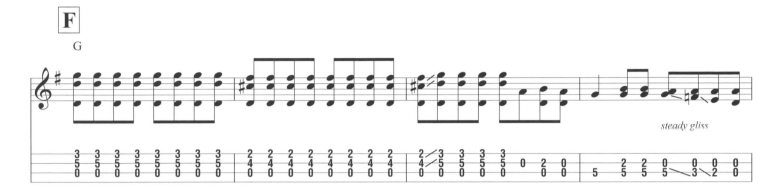

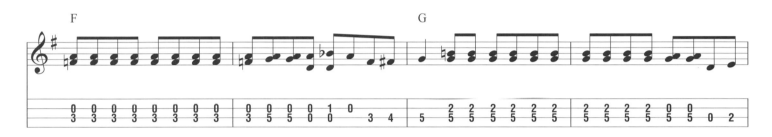

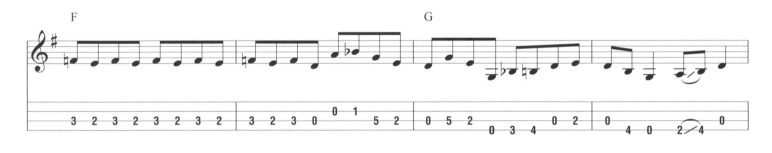

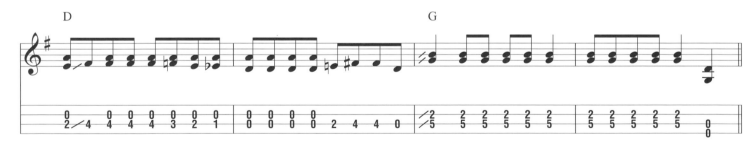

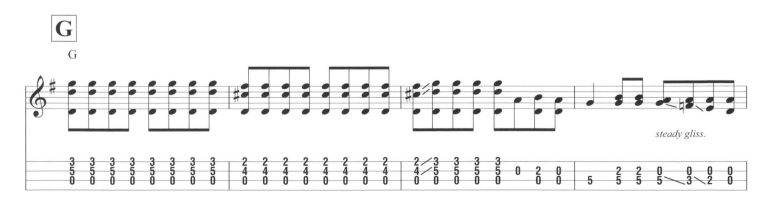

11

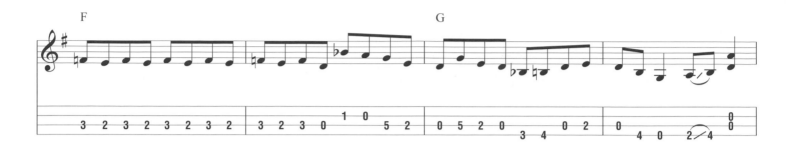

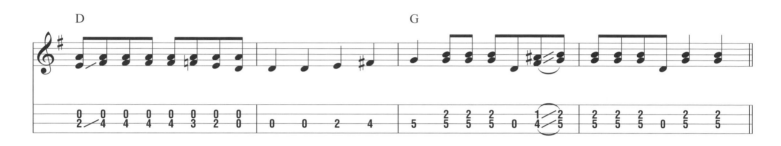

H

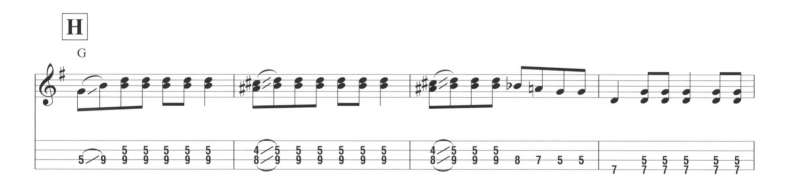

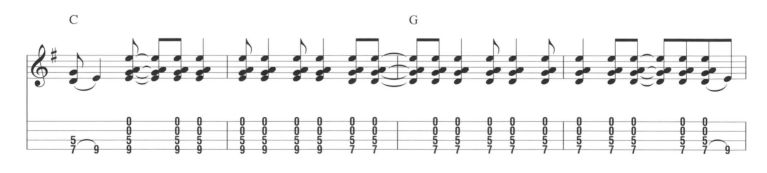

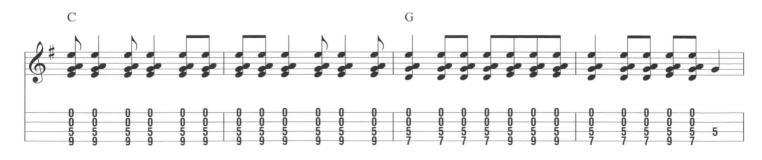

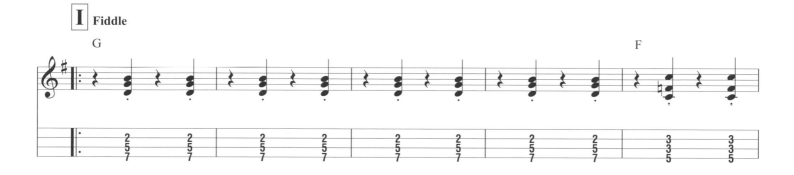

I Fiddle

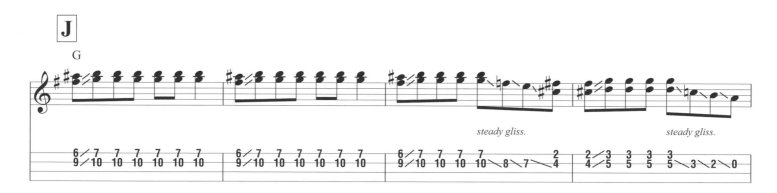

J

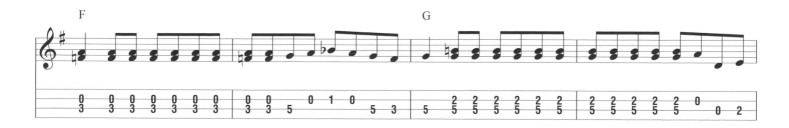

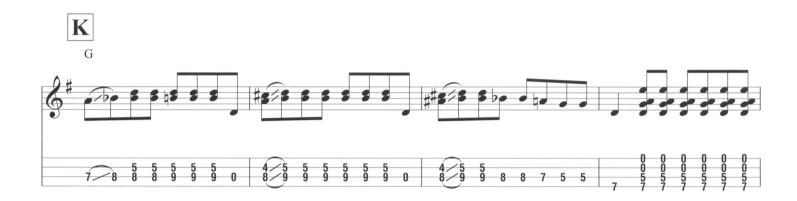

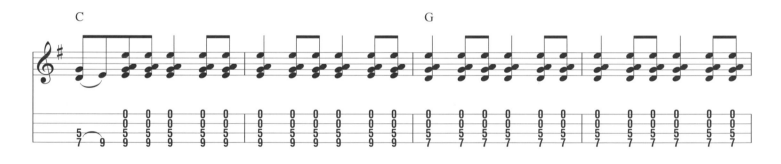

Blue Moon of Kentucky

Words and Music by Bill Monroe

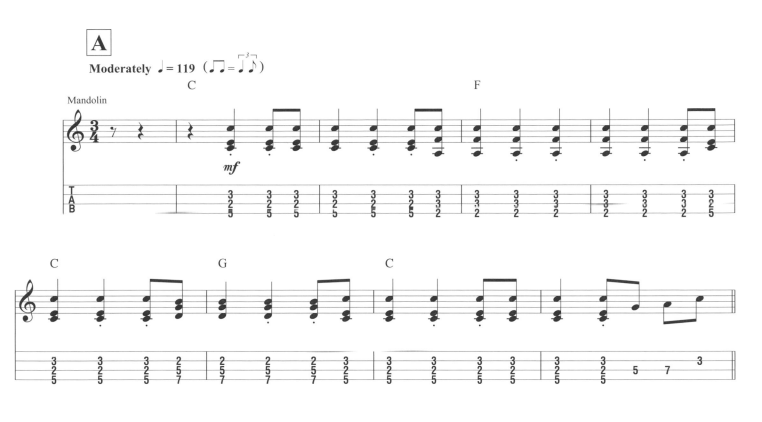

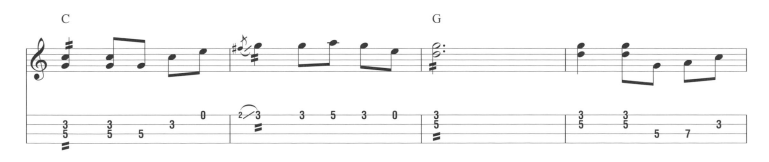

Copyright © 1946 Bill Monroe Music, Inc.
Copyright Renewed
All Rights in the United States Administered by BMG Rights Management (US) LLC
All Rights Reserved   Used by Permission

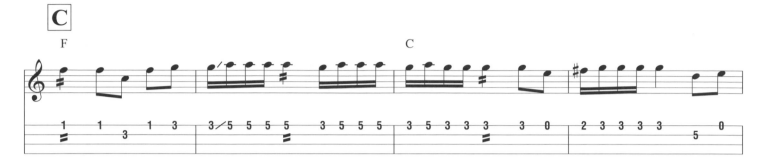

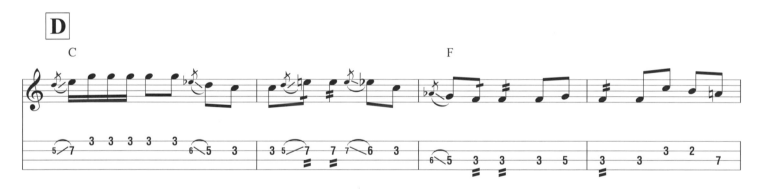

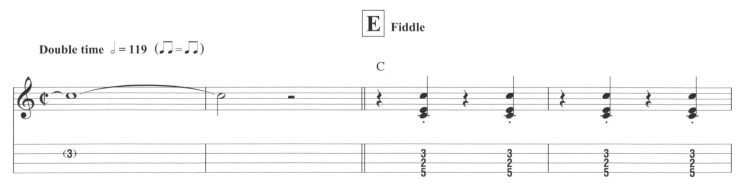

16

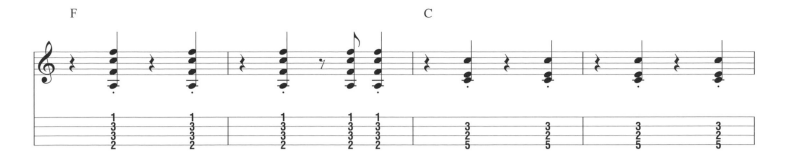

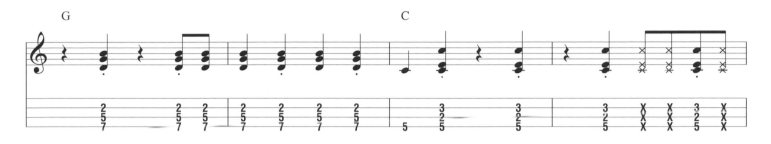

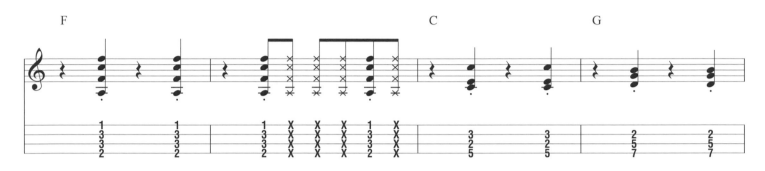

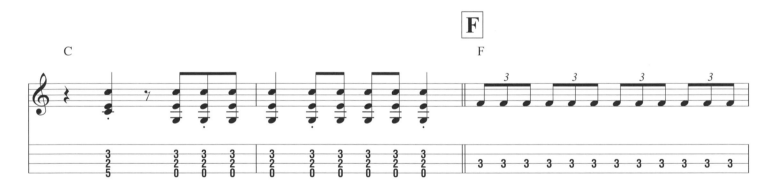

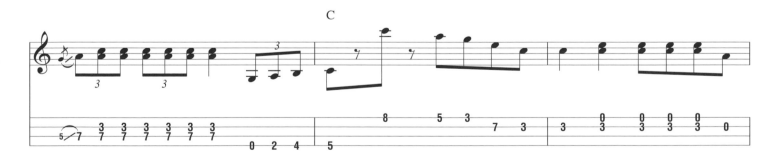

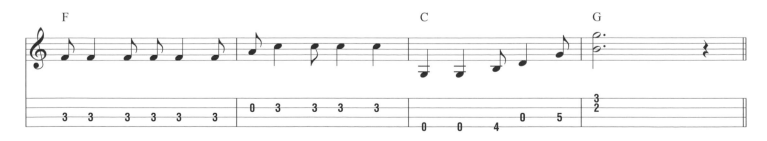

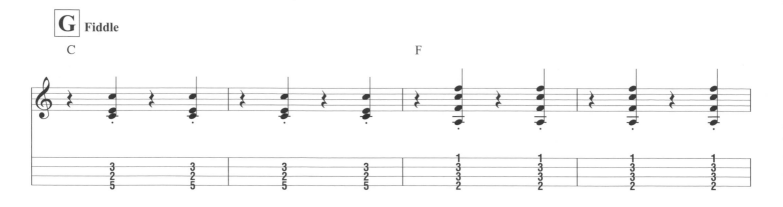

G Fiddle

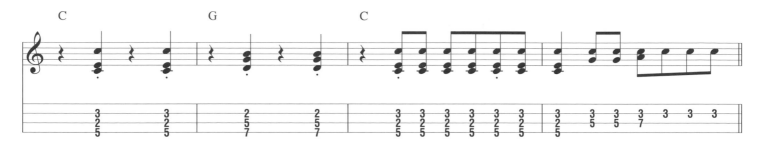

H

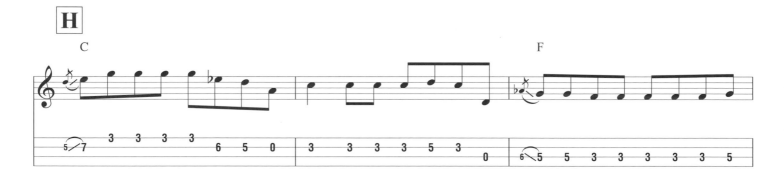

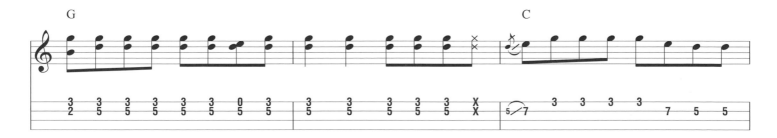

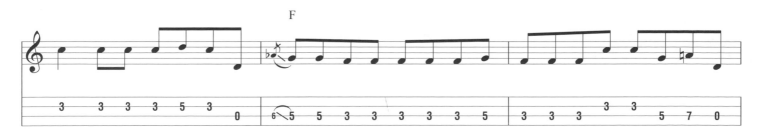

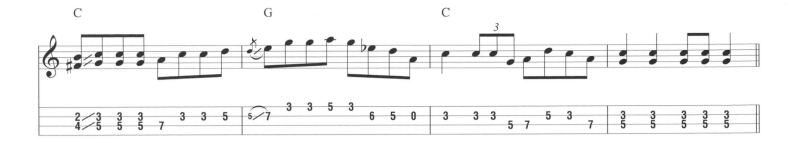

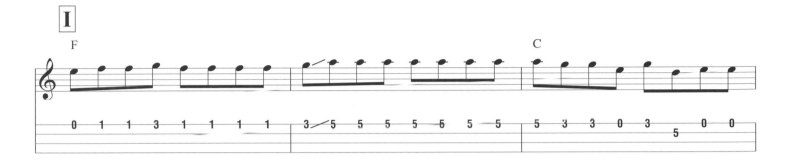

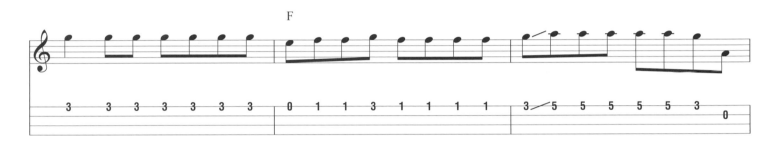

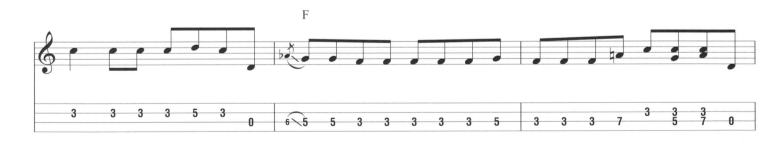

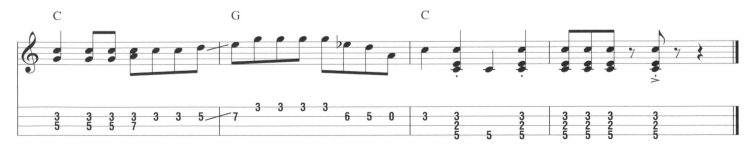

Get Up John

Words and Music by Bill Monroe

Tuning:
(low to high) F♯A-DD-AA-AD

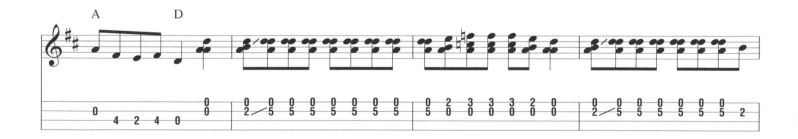

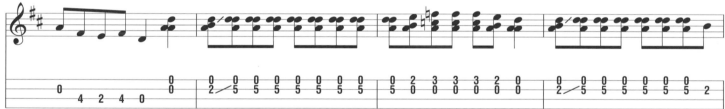

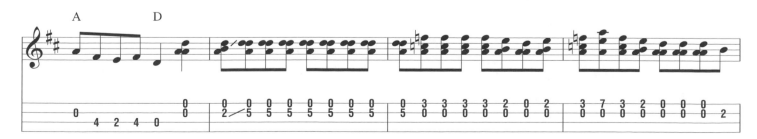

© 1954 (Renewed) UNICHAPPELL MUSIC, INC.
All Rights Reserved   Used by Permission

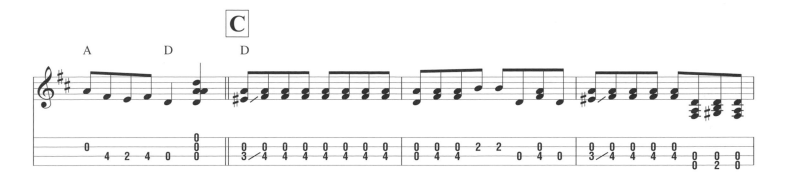

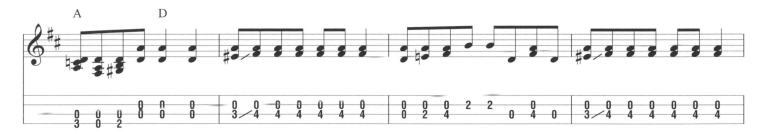

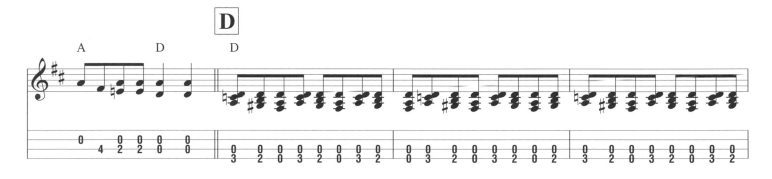

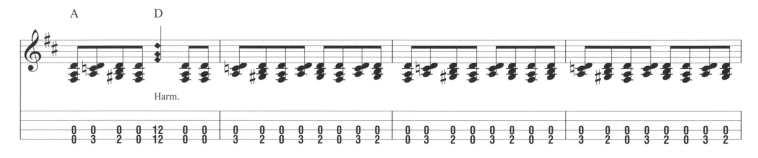

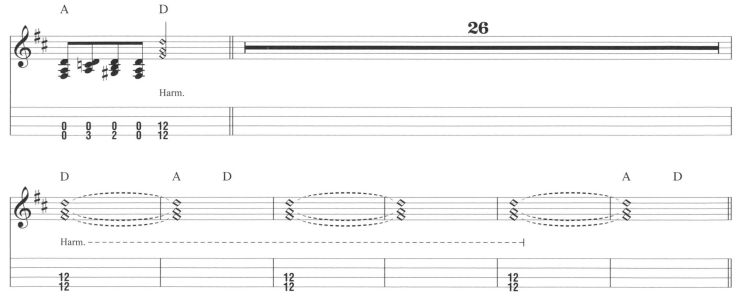

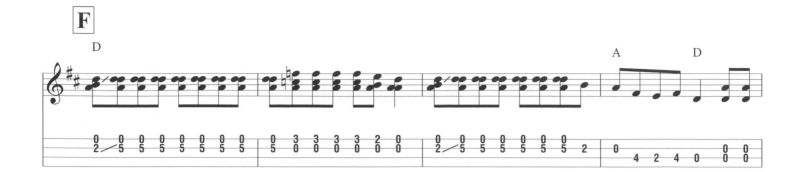

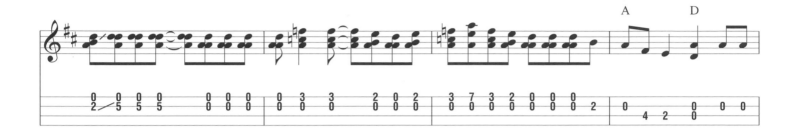

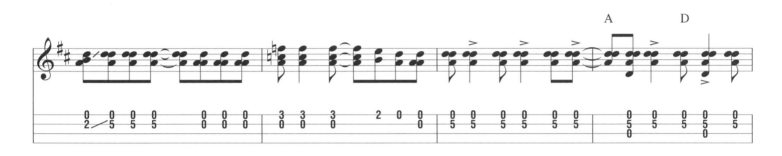

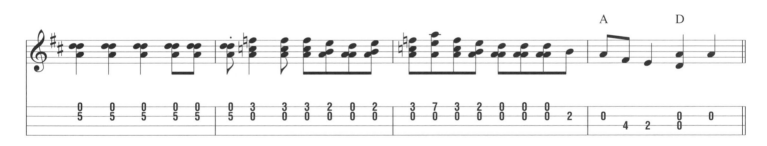

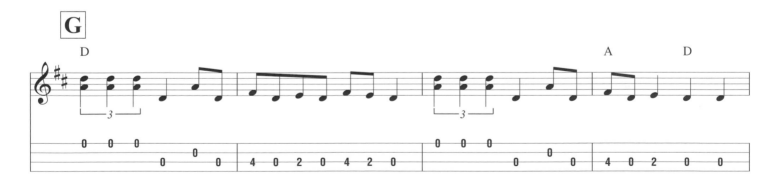

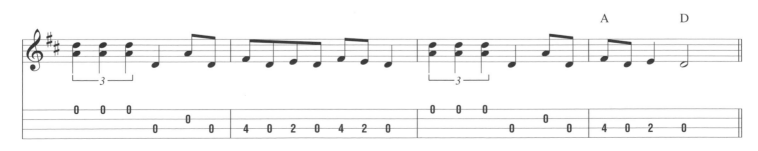

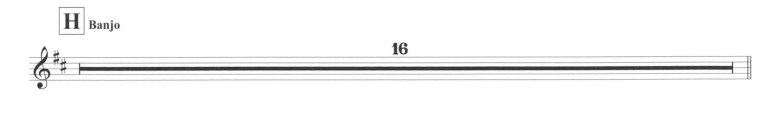

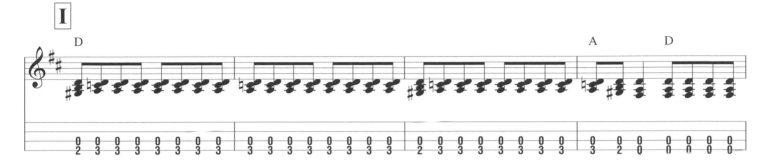

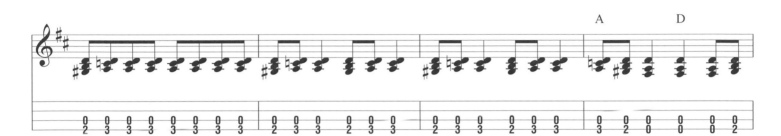

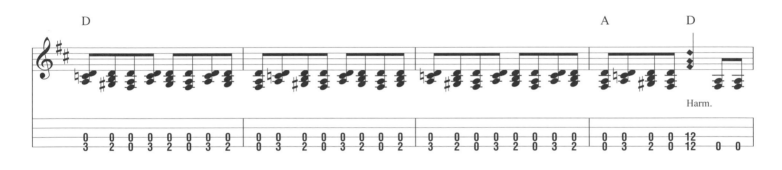

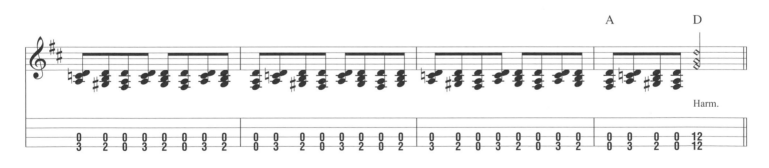

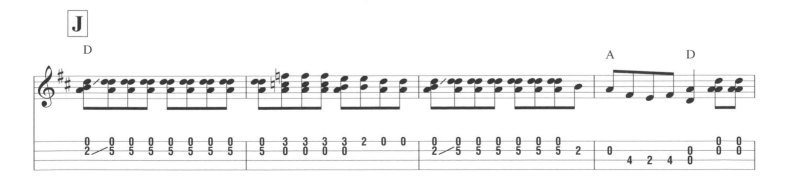

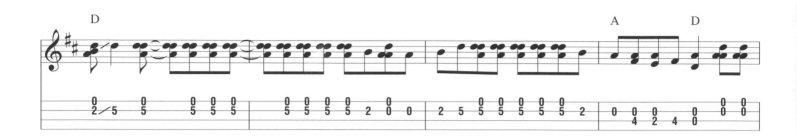

K

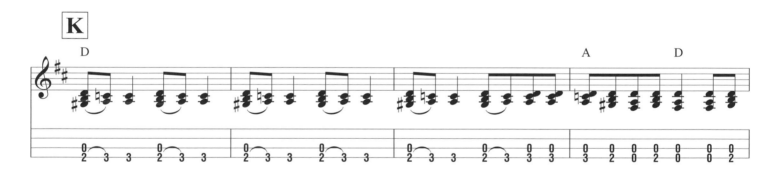

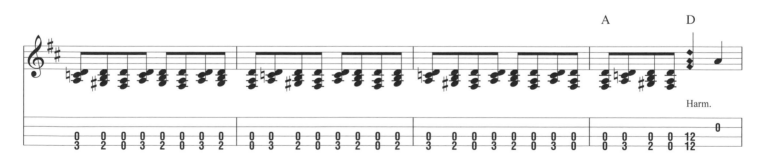

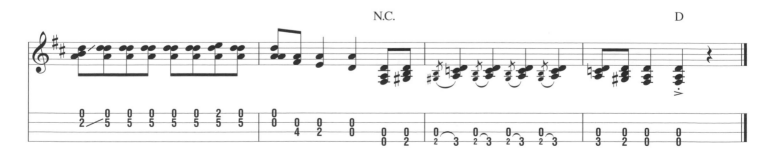

Kentucky Mandolin

Words and Music by Bill Monroe

Copyright © 1975 Bill Monroe Music, Inc.
Copyright Renewed
All Rights in the United States Administered by BMG Rights Management (US) LLC
All Rights Reserved   Used by Permission

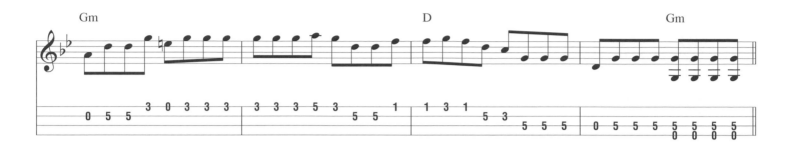

D

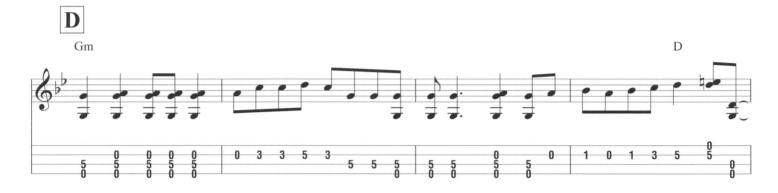

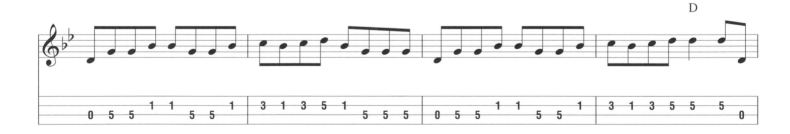

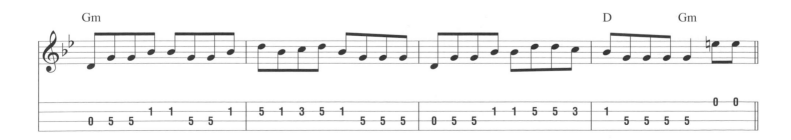

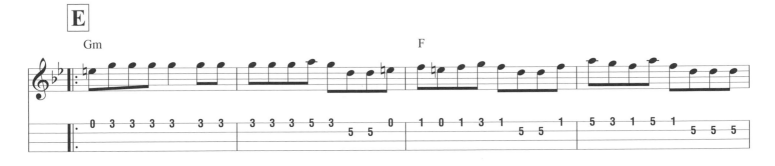

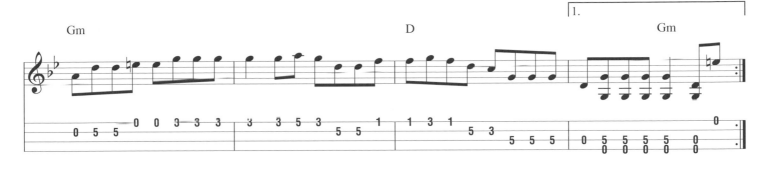

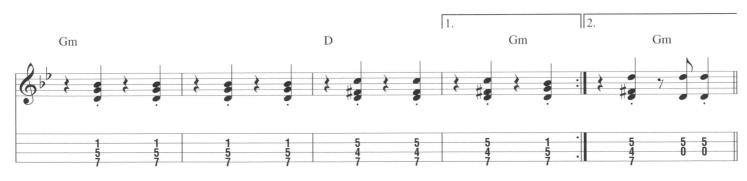

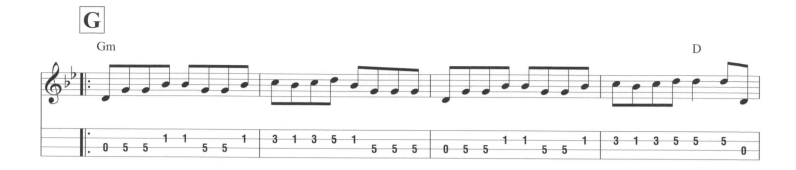

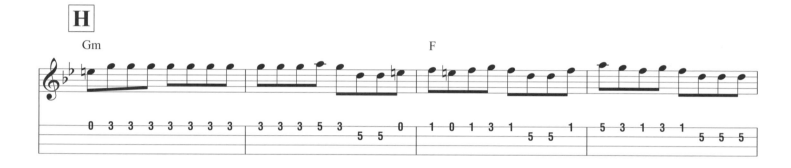

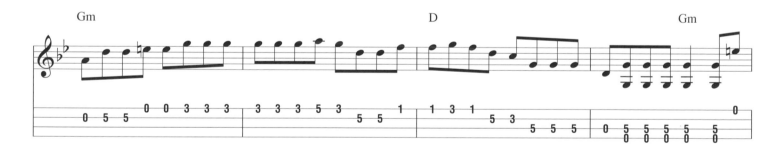

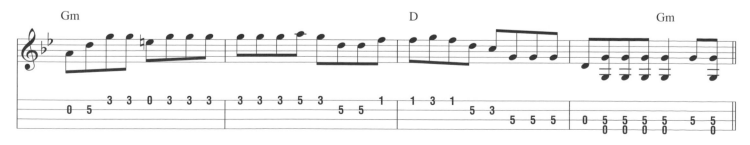

I Fiddle

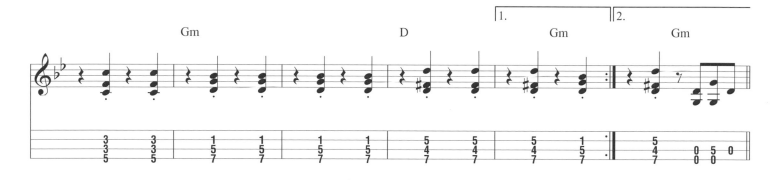

J

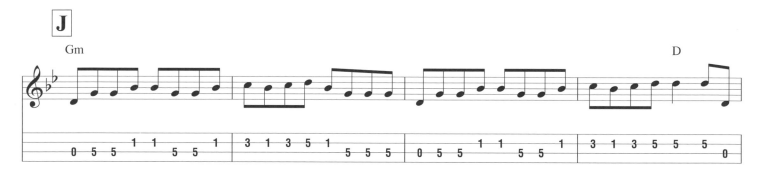

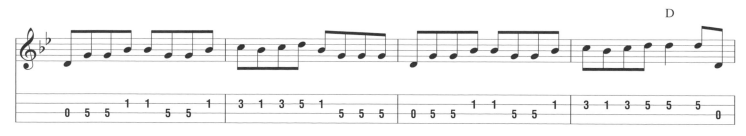

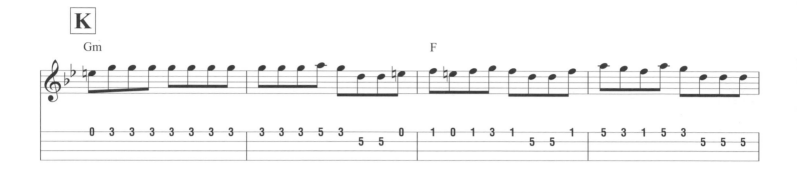

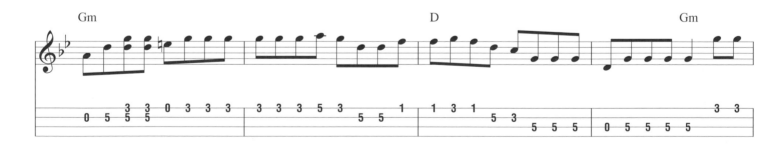

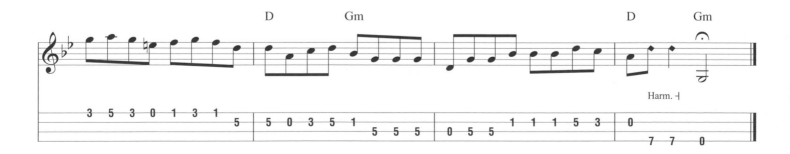

My Last Days on Earth

Words and Music by Bill Monroe

*Lightly touch fret-hand finger to strings just in front of the nut and strike to produce muted notes w/ overtones.

Copyright © 1981 Bill Monroe Music, Inc.
All Rights Administered by BMG Rights Management (US) LLC
All Rights Reserved   Used by Permission

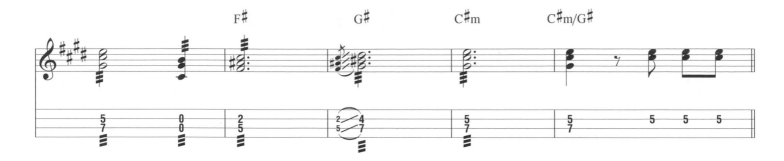

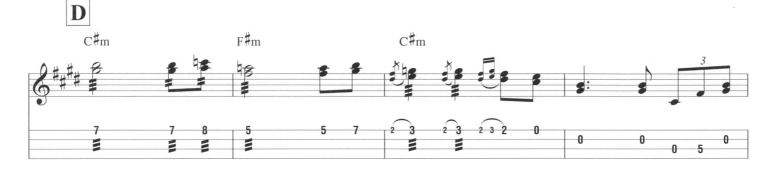

D

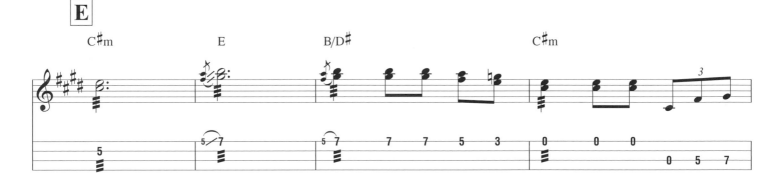

E

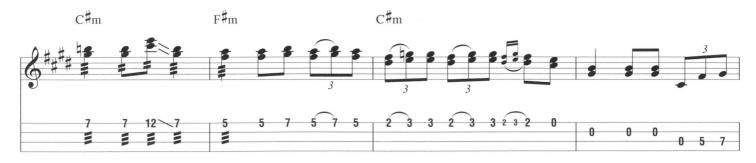

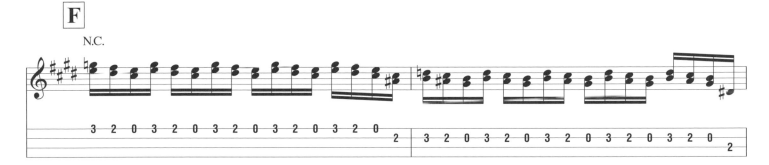

F

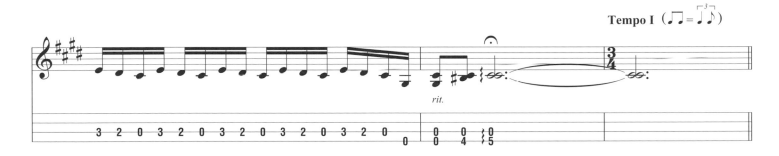

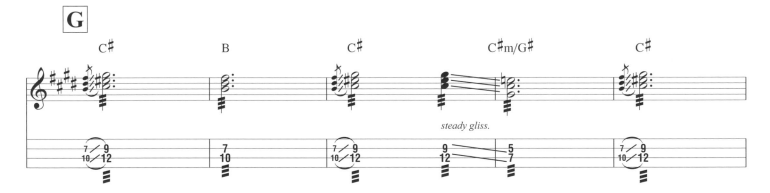

G

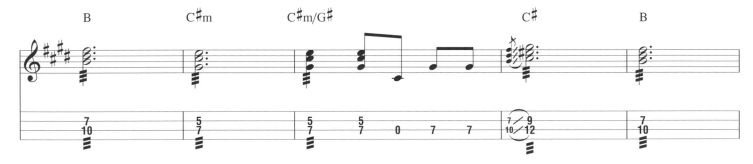

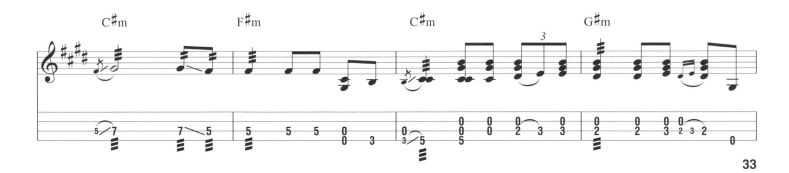

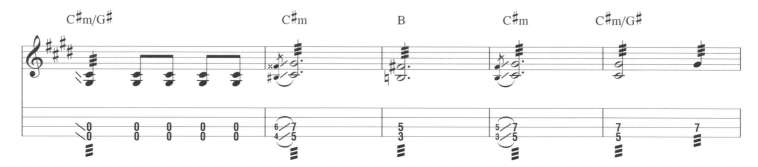

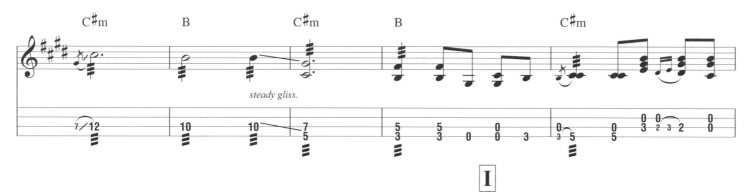

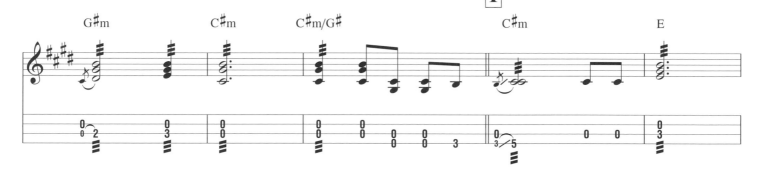

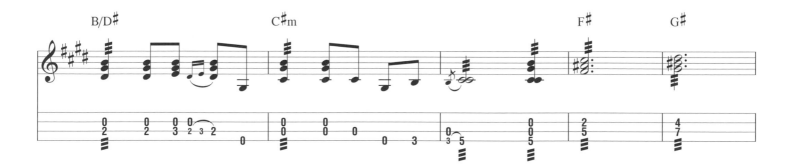

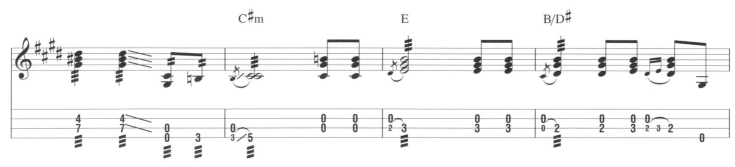

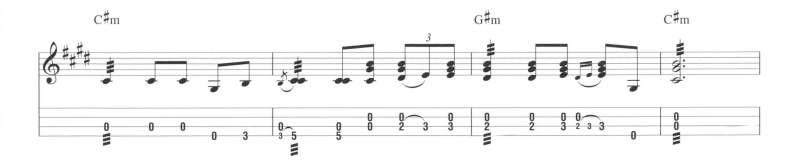

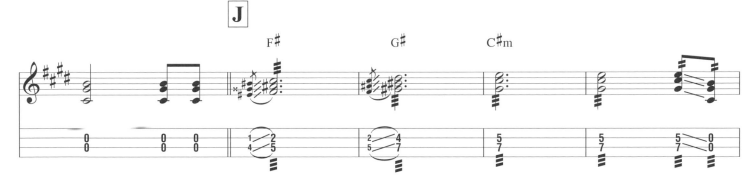

J

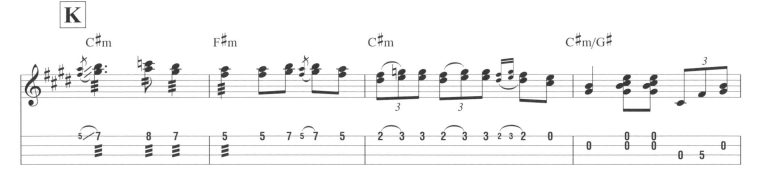

K

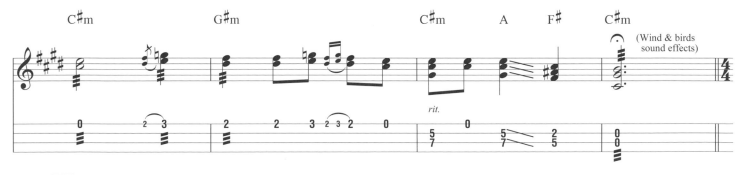

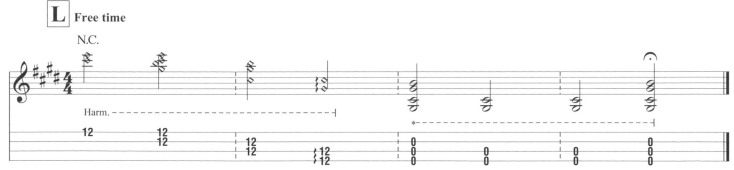

L **Free time**

Lightly touch fret-hand finger to strings, as before.

Raw Hide

Words and Music by Bill Monroe

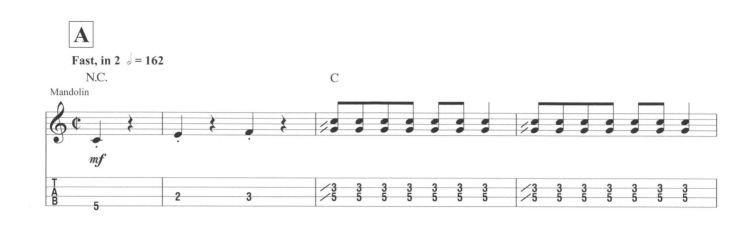

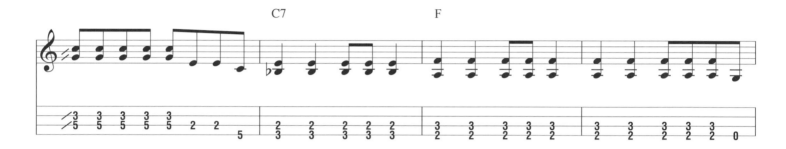

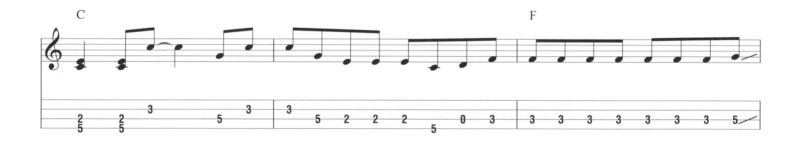

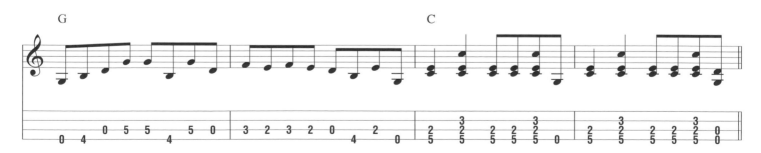

Copyright © 1952 Bill Monroe Music, Inc.
Copyright Renewed
All Rights Administered by BMG Rights Management (US) LLC
All Rights Reserved   Used by Permission

B

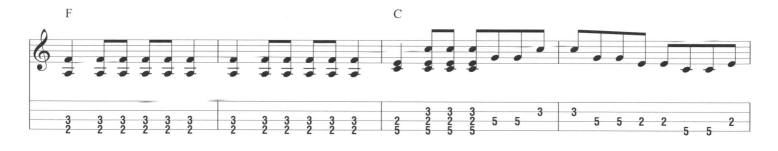

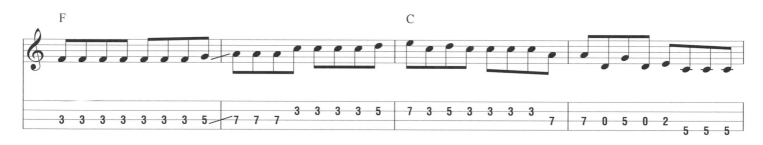

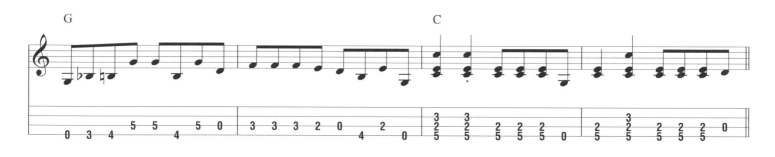

C

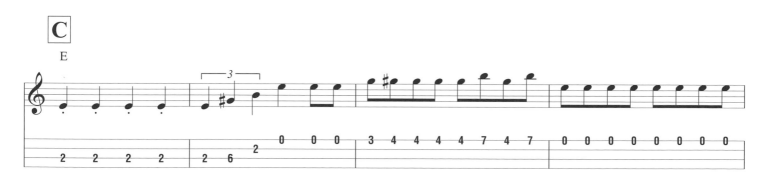

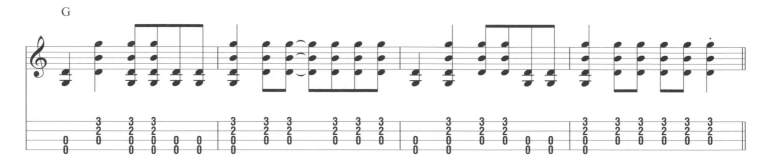

D Fiddle

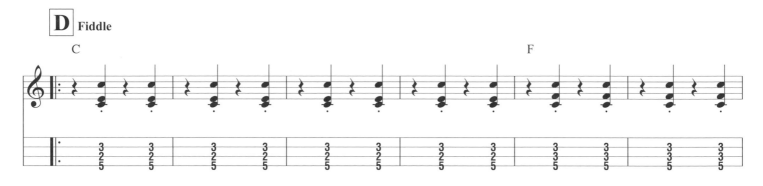

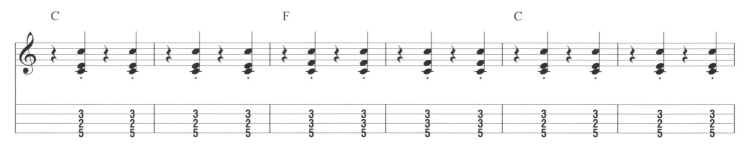

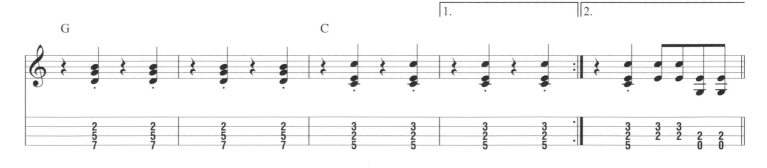

E

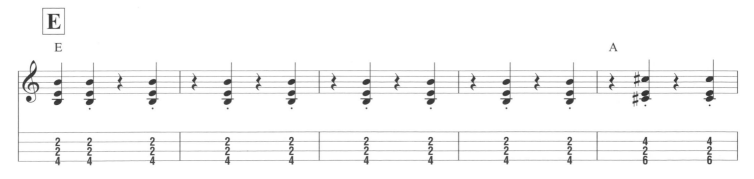

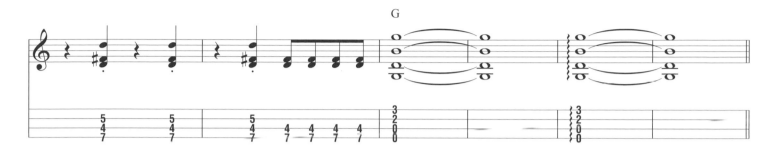

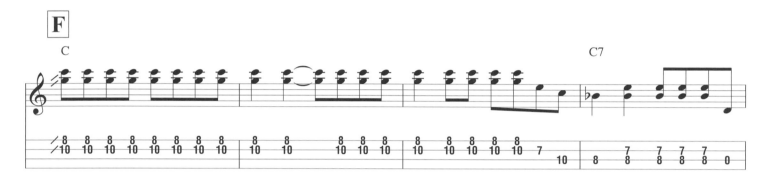

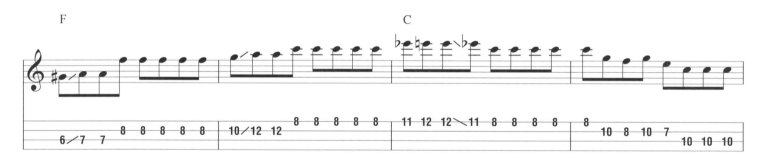

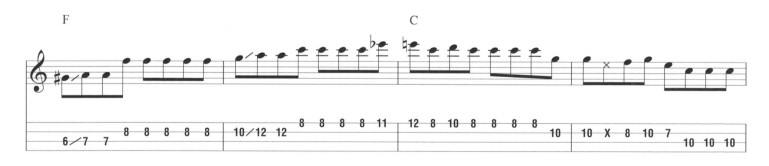

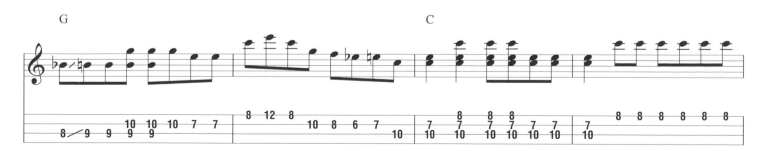

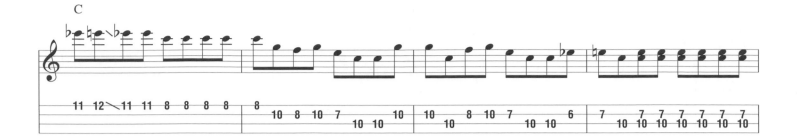

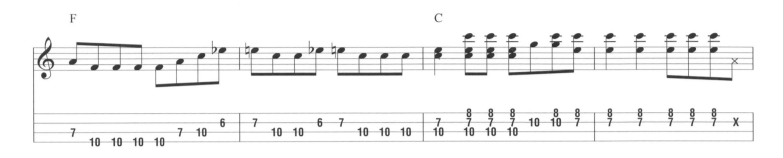

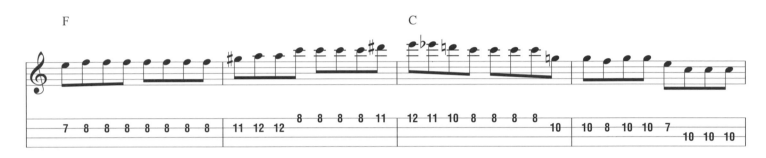

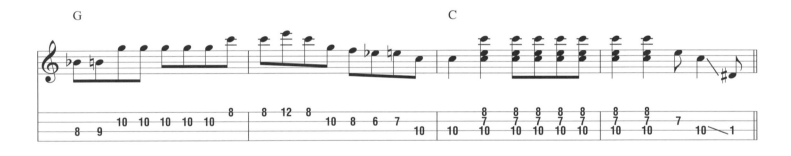

G

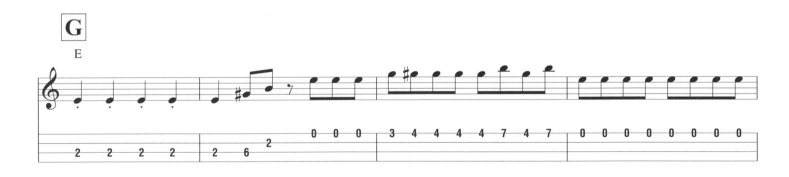

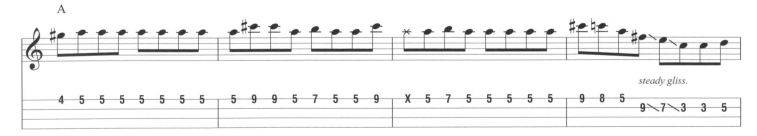

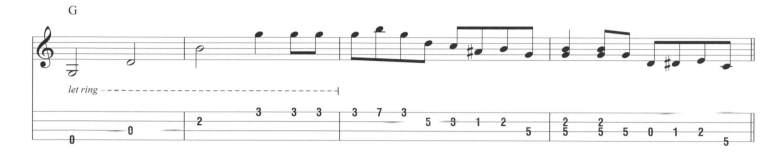

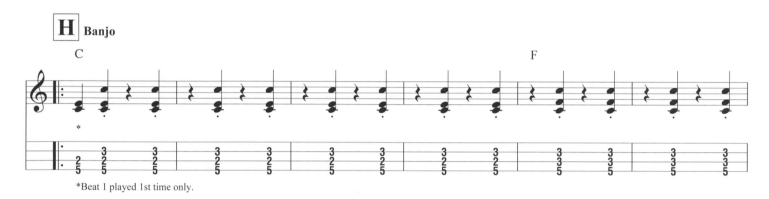

*Beat 1 played 1st time only.

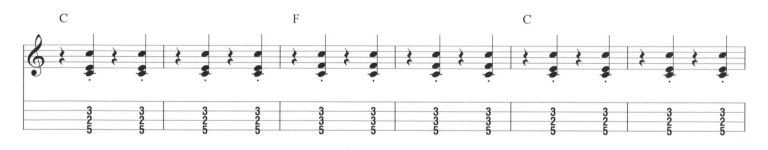

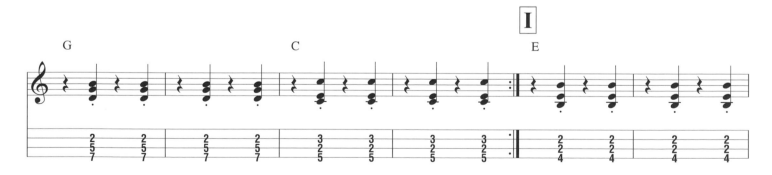

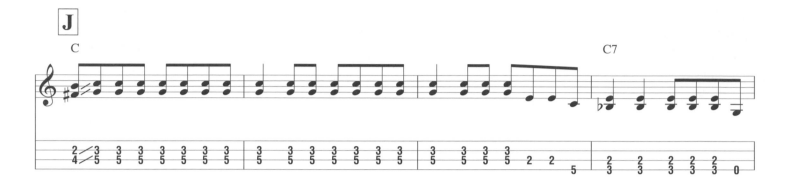

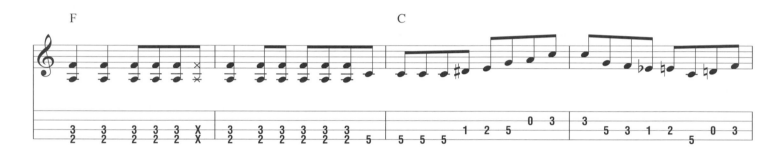

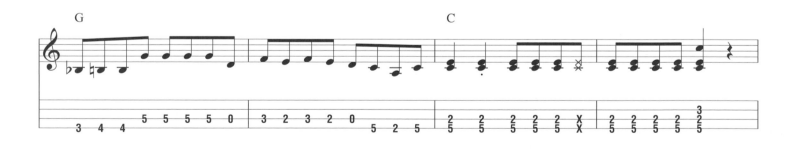

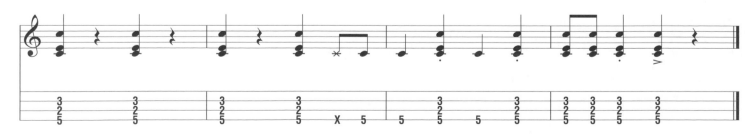

Roanoke

Words and Music by Joe Ahr

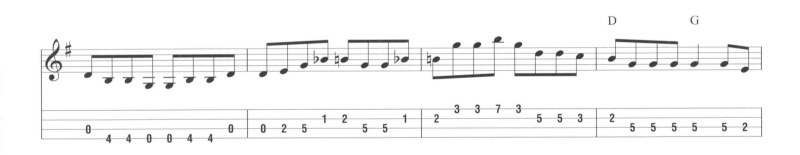

© 1955 (Renewed) UNICHAPPELL MUSIC, INC.
All Rights Reserved   Used by Permission

C

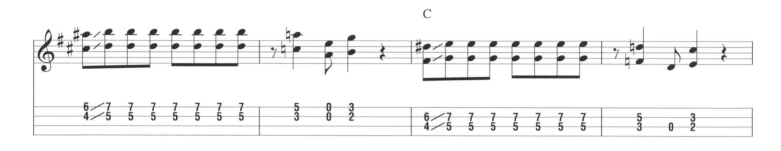

D

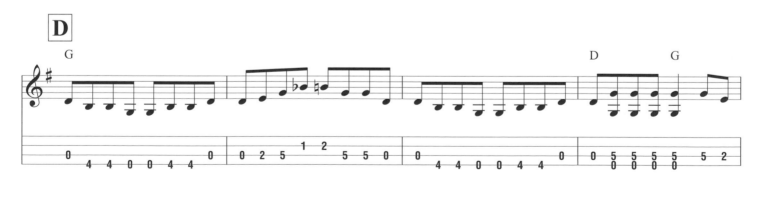

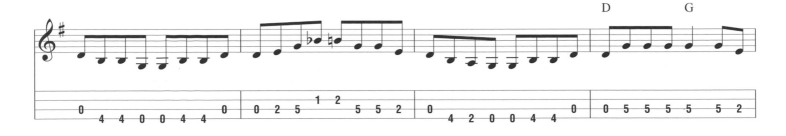

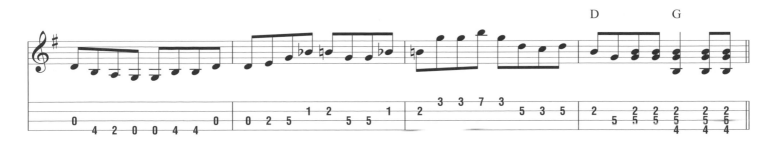

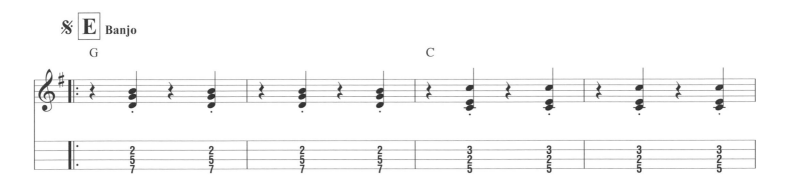

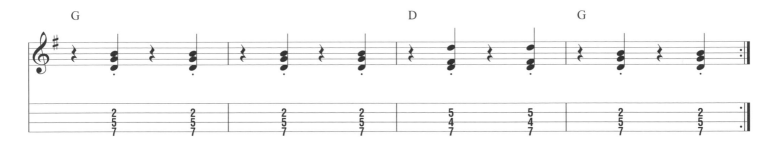

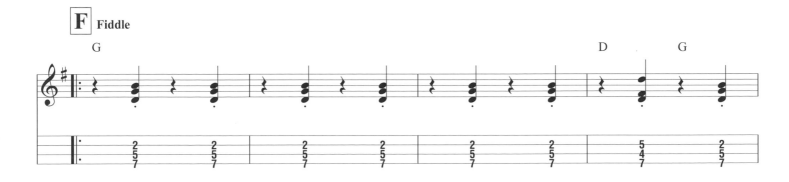

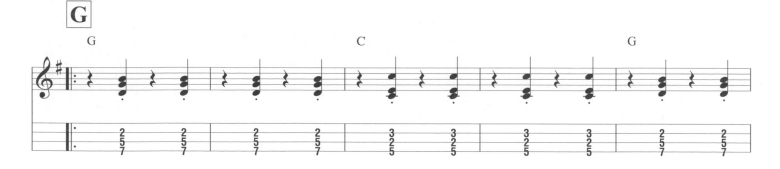

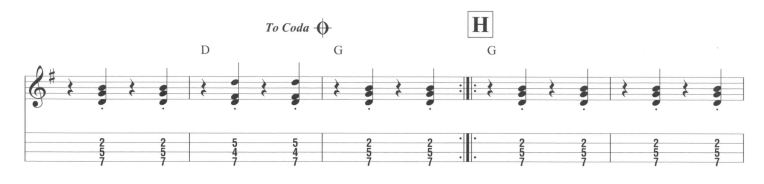

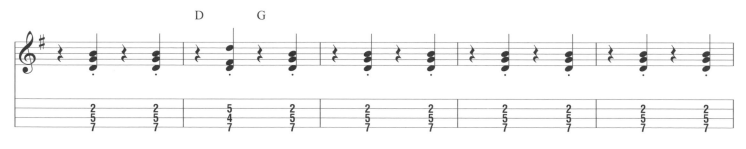

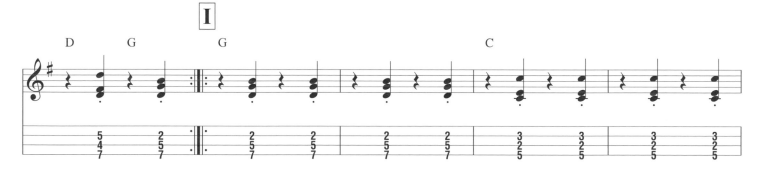

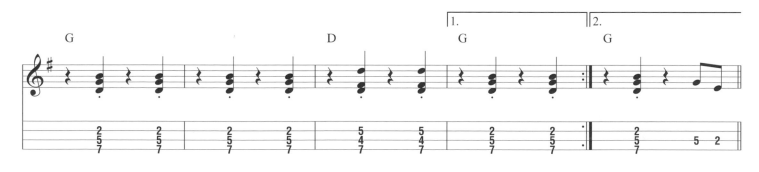

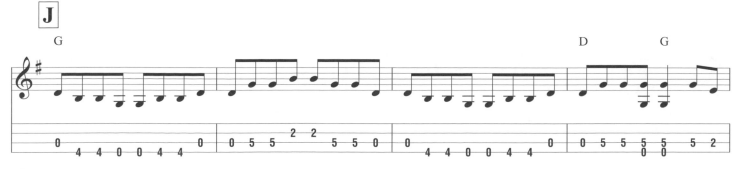

D.S. al Coda

⊕ Coda

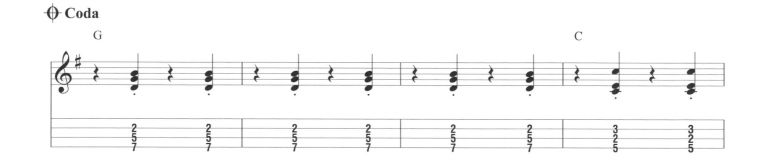

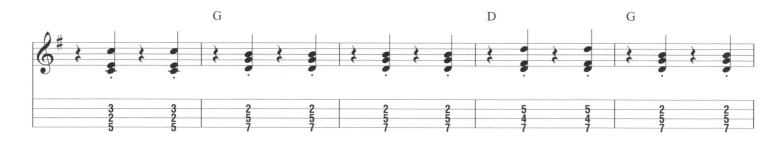

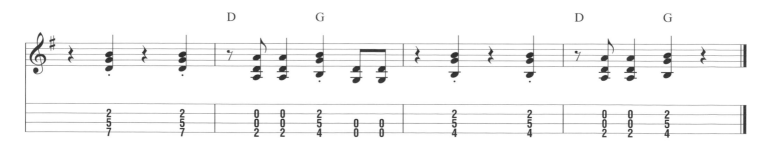

MANDOLIN NOTATION LEGEND

Mandolin music can be notated three different ways: on a *musical staff*, in *tablature*, and in *rhythm slashes*.

RHYTHM SLASHES are written above the staff. Strum chords in the rhythm indicated. Use the chord diagrams found at the top of the first page of the transcription for the appropriate chord voicings.

THE MUSICAL STAFF shows pitches and rhythms and is divided by bar lines into measures. Pitches are named after the first seven letters of the alphabet.

TABLATURE graphically represents the mandolin fretboard. Each of the four horizontal lines represents each of the four courses of strings, and each number represents a fret.

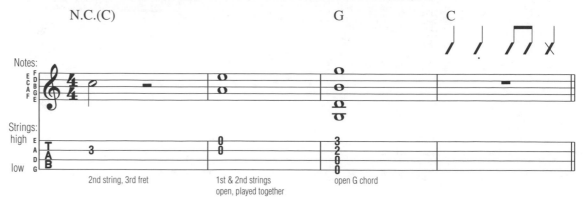

2nd string, 3rd fret

1st & 2nd strings open, played together

open G chord

Definitions for Special Mandolin Notation

MUTED STRING(S): Lightly touch a string with the edge of your fret-hand finger while fretting a note on an adjacent string, causing the muted string to be unheard. Muting all of the strings with the fingers of the fret-hand while strumming the strings with the picking hand produces a percussive effect.

HAMMER-ON: Strike the first (lower) note with one finger, then sound the higher note (on the same string) with another finger by fretting it without picking.

PULL-OFF: Place both fingers on the notes to be sounded. Strike the first note and, without picking, pull the finger off to sound the second (lower) note.

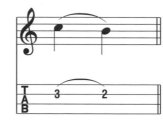

LEGATO SLIDE: Strike the first note and then slide the same fret-hand finger up or down to the second note. The second note is not struck.

SHIFT SLIDE: Same as the legato slide except the second note is struck.

HALF-STEP BEND: Strike the note and bend up ½ step.

GRACE NOTE BEND: Strike the note and immediately bend up as indicated.

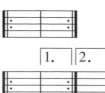

TREMOLO PICKING: The note is picked rapidly and continuously.

Additional Musical Definitions

p *(piano)*	• Play quietly.	
mp *(mezzo-piano)*	• Play moderately quiet.	
mf *(mezzo-forte)*	• Play moderately loud.	
f *(forte)*	• Play loudly.	
cont. rhy. sim.	• Continue strumming in similar rhythm.	
N.C. *(no chord)*	• Don't strum until the next chord symbol. Chord symbols in parentheses reflect implied harmony.	
D.S. al Coda	• Go back to the sign (𝄋), then play until the measure marked *"To Coda"*, then skip to the section labeled *"Coda."*	
D.S.S. al Coda 2	• Go back to the double sign (𝄋𝄋), then play until the measure marked *"To Coda 2"*, then skip to the section labeled *"Coda 2."*	
D.S. al Fine	• Go back to the sign (𝄋), then play until the label *"Fine."*	

(staccato) • Play the note or chord short.

rit. *(ritard)* • Gradually slow down.

(fermata) • Hold the note or chord for an undetermined amount of time.

• Repeat measures between signs.

1. **2.** • When a repeated section has different endings, play the first ending only the first time and the second ending only the second time.

NOTE: Tablature numbers in parentheses mean:
1. The note is being sustained over a system (note in standard notation is tied), or
2. The note is sustained, but a new articulation (such as a hammer-on, pull-off or slide) begins.